Can't wait
to meet you :)

❀ ❀ ❀

To:

Baby Kemppainen

May you be blessed by the Lord,
the Maker of heaven and earth.

Psalm 115:15

From:

Krista Cannon + Marissa

God Bless Your Baby
Copyright 2002 by Zondervan
ISBN 0310-80311-X

Compiler: Molly C. Detweiler
Designer: Kris Nelson
Illustrations: Karen Clark

Printed in China
03 04 05/ HK/5 4 3 2 1

God Bless Your Baby

inspirio™

The gift group of Zondervan

$\mathcal{B}$aby, you came down from God

$\mathcal{A}$nd nestled in our hearts.

$\mathcal{B}$undle of joy,

$\mathcal{Y}$ou are our priceless treasure!

Conover Swofford

Every good and perfect gift is from above,
coming down from the Father of heavenly lights,
who does not change like shifting shadows.

James 1:17

I love these little people;
and it is not a slight thing when they,
who are so fresh from God, love us.

Charles Dickens

Lullaby Town

There's a quaint little place they call
Lullaby Town—
It's just back of those hills where
the sunsets go down.

Its streets are of silver,
its buildings of gold,
And its palaces dazzling
things to behold;

There are dozens of spires,
housing musical chimes;
Its people are folk from
the Nursery Rhymes,

And at night it's alight,
like a garden of gleams,
With angels, who bring
the most wonderful dreams.

John Irving Diller

Jesus ... took a little child and had him
stand beside him. Then he said to [his disciples],
"Whoever welcomes this little child in my
name welcomes me; and whoever welcomes me
welcomes the one who sent me."

Luke 9:47–48

God makes us babies so that
we fit in our mother's stomach.
And he puts good food in there
that only babies like.

Brent Glover, age 8

God gives me a sister to love
and it helps me learn to be nice.

Kelsi Wilson, age 6

God makes us headfirst
and then he adds body and legs.
And last he reaches inside his own body
and puts some soul in us.

Jack Finlay, age 6

Many, O Lord my God,
are the wonders you have done.
The things you planned for us
no one can recount to you;
were I to speak and tell of them,
they would be too many to declare.

Psalm 40:5

I kiss her chilly hands and that little rounded
forehead. I squeeze her chubby cheeks and legs.
She giggles and grabs my nose. These are the
moments that will last forever in my memory—
Or at least until the next really cute thing she does.

God has
brought
me laughter.

Genesis 21:6

A Prayer for Baby

May you always be aware of
the beauty around you even in the
seemingly mundane events of life.
May you be blessed with family
and teachers who allow you to
express yourself and help guide
you in your special talents.
And may you grow into the
knowledge that you are God's
child, always surrounded by his
love, his care, and his peace.
Amen.

All your sons will be taught by the Lord,
and great will be your children's peace.

Isaiah 54:13

Like arrows in the hands of a warrior
are sons born in one's youth.
Blessed is the man whose quiver is full of them.

Psalm 127:4-5

You brought me out of the womb, O Lord;
you made me trust in you even at my mother's breast.

Psalm 22:9

Little Lamb Who Made Thee?

❋ ❋ ❋

Little Lamb, who made thee?

Dost thou know who made thee?

Gave thee life and beg thee feed

By the stream and o'er the mead;

Gave thee clothing of delight,

Softest clothing, woolly, bright.

Little Lamb, I'll tell thee,

Little Lamb I'll tell thee:

He is called by thy name

For he calls himself a Lamb.

He is meek and he is mild;

He became a little child.

I a child, and thou a lamb,

We are called by his name.

Little Lamb, God bless thee!

Little Lamb, God bless thee!

William Blake

Every child is
God's miracle.

Philip Bailey

Sons are a heritage
from the Lord,
children a reward
from him.

Psalm 127:3

A Prayer for Bath Time

❀ ❀ ❀

I wash the dirt from off two feet,
and as I wash I pray,
Lord, keep them ever pure
and true to walk the narrow way.
I wash the dirt from little hands,
and earnestly I ask,
Lord, may they ever yielded be
to do the humblest task.
I wash the dirt from soiled knees,
and pray, Lord, may they be
The place where victories are won,
and orders sought from thee.

B. Ryberg

little love
    tiny toes
        mama's eyes
            daddy's nose

beautiful baby
    pure, smooth skin
        please won't you stay
            innocent within?

We are God's workmanship,
created in Christ Jesus to do good works.

Ephesians 2:10

All Night, All Day

Angels watching over me, my Lord.
All night, all day,
Angels watching over me.

Sun is a-setting in the West;
Angels watching over me, my Lord.
Sleep my child, take your rest;
Angels watching over me.

All night, all day,
Angels watching over me, my Lord.
All night, all day,
Angels watching over me.

Traditional American Folk Song

My Child

It was a night I won't forget
When you came into my life;
A miracle was right before my eyes.
This little baby girl
Would steal my heart away,
And I was left with just one thing to say …

You are my child,
A precious one;
You are a miracle of God's unending love.
You are my child,
And now it's plain to see
How great a love the Father has for me.

As I lay you down to sleep
With the angels at your side,
I pray that you would give your heart away
To the One who chose to die,
Who loved you with his life.
And just for you He'd do it all again.

You are my child,
A precious one;
You are a miracle of God's unending love.
You are my child,
And now it's plain to see
How great a love the Father has for me.

Dan Klotz

God has blessed my child with time.
I pray he will use it wisely.
For if he takes time to work, he will find success.
If he takes time to play, he will stay young.
If he takes time to read, wisdom will be his.
If he takes time for friends, he will be happy.
If he takes time to worship, he will find strength.
But if he takes time to love and be loved,
and he will find God.

The Lord tends his flock like a shepherd:
He gathers the lambs in his arms
and carries them close to his heart;
He gently leads those that have young.

Isaiah 40:11

A new baby
is like the beginning
of all things—
wonder, hope, a dream
of possibilities.

Eda J. Leshan

You created my inmost being, Lord;
you knit me together in my mother's womb.
I praise you because I am fearfully
and wonderfully made;
your works are wonderful,
I know that full well.
My frame was not hidden from you
when I was made in the secret place.
When I was woven together
in the depths of the earth,
your eyes saw my unformed body.
All the days ordained for me were
written in your book
before one of them came to be.

Psalm 139:13–16

The heart of a child is
the most precious of
God's creation.

Joseph L. Whitten

Dear God, remind my child that you made her
the way she is. You knit her together into a child
that is fearfully and wonderfully made. Amen.

"Before I formed you in the womb I knew you,
before you were born I set you apart," says the Lord.

Jeremiah 1:5

The Goodnight Angel

The goodnight angel comes at eve

Across the quiet hills,

And tucks the sleepy blossoms in

Beside the meadow's rills.

On uplands wide each drowsy bird

He cradles in its nest,

And in the dewy valley far

He rocks wild winds to rest.

He pauses in his gracious guise

Where little children play,

And blesses each before he speeds

Upon his kindly way;

And ere he passes back to heaven

Beyond the sunset bars,

To watch the babies, birds and buds,

For lamps he lights the stars.

Lucy Maud Montgomery

The Lord will keep
you from all harm—
he will watch over your life;
the Lord will watch over
your coming and going
both now and forevermore.

Psalm 121:7–8

As I look at my little one, I find myself wondering
for the millionth time how anyone could be so
beautiful, so perfect. Everything about this child
seems miraculous to me; every motion, every sound
is significant. Nothing is too small to be wondrous.

Cradle Song

Sweet babe, in thy face

Soft desires I can trace,

Secret joys and secret smiles,

Little pretty infant wiles.

As thy softest limbs I feel

Smiles as of the morning steal

O'er thy cheek, and o'er thy breast

Where thy little heart doth rest.

William Blake

Sharing a quiet moment with my baby
is like heaven on earth to me.
Smelling the clean, soft skin of a newborn,
listening to the deep, gentle breathing
of a peaceful slumber. ...
What more is there to life than
this kind of silent pleasure?

May your father
and mother be glad;
may she who gave
you birth rejoice!

Proverbs 23:25

Wonder

What a wonder you've made, God!

Eyes that can see the unseen.

Ears that can hear innermost thoughts.

A mouth that can bestow blessings

or swallow hurts before they

have injured another.

Hands that can carry

immeasurable burdens.

A heart that can beat with divine love.

A mind that can believe

and learn and grow.

What a wonder you've made!

What a wonder I am!

Francis Thompson

What is a Baby?

A baby is a soft little hand,

curling warmly around your finger.

A baby is a lively little pair of legs,

kicking happily in the air after a bath.

A baby is a puckered and trembling lower lip,

trying hard, oh so hard, to tell you something.

A baby is a cry in the night,

calling you swiftly out of sleep

and to its crib.

A baby is an eloquent pair of eyes,

one time dancing with glee …

another time staring at you

with sober reflection.

But above all a baby is a priceless

gift from God.

Those little hands must learn to move

in his service; those little feet must

grow up to walk in his ways;

and those little eyes must learn

to focus on his Word.

Author Unknown

Baby Shoes

Often tiny baby feet,
Tired from their play,
Kick off scuffed-up little shoes
At the close of day.
And often tired mothers
Find them lying there,
And over them send up to God
This fervent, whispered prayer:
God guide their every footstep
In paths where thou hast stood;
God, make them brave;
God, make them strong;
And please, God, make them good!

Mary Holmes

What a joy and
precious gem you are,
my child!
A gift from God
I've just barely
begun to open.

Where Did You Come From, Baby Dear?

Where did you come from, baby dear?

Out of the everywhere into here.

Where did you get your eyes so blue?

Out of the sky as I came through.

Where did you get this pearly ear?

God spoke, and it came out to hear.

But how did you come to us, you dear?

God thought about you, and so I am here.

George MacDonald

The Lord your God is with you,
he is mighty to save.
He will take great delight in you,
he will quiet you with his love,
he will rejoice over you with singing.

Zephaniah 3:17

God has presented me
with a precious gift.

Genesis 30:20

Babies bring us to a new awareness.
Many things we took for granted become
small wonders: The wonder of growing ...
of moving ... of touching ... and smiling!

Susan Squellati Florence

Every child born into the world is a new thought
of God, an ever-fresh and radiant possibility.

Kate Douglas Wiggin

Everything about you is so little—
your tiny toes, your button nose, your teensy fingers
and your pint-sized giggles.
And yet, you are the biggest miracle of my life!

Author Unknown

I see the sunshine in your smile.
You mean so much,
my precious child.
I'm here to help you
learn and grow,
And share with you
the things I know.
But most of all
I hope that you
Will love God
'cause he loves you too.

Jesus said, "Let the little children come to me, and do not hinder them, for the kingdom of heaven belongs to such as these."

Matthew 19:14

Every baby born into the world is a finer one than the last.

Charles Dickens

Dear child, you are one of a kind! You are a special gift from God in packaging that is all your own. My prayer is that you will celebrate that today and always—just as your mommy and daddy do!

Londa Alderink

Come, my children, come away,
For the sun shines bright today;
Little children, come with me,
Birds and brooks and posies see;
Get your hats and come away,
For it is a pleasant day.

Everything is laughing, singing,
All the pretty flowers are springing;
See the kitten, full of fun,
Sporting in the brilliant sun;
Children too may sport and play,
For it is a pleasant day.

Bring the jump rope, bring the ball,
Come with happy faces all;
Let us make a merry ring,
Talk and laugh, and dance and sing.
Quickly, quickly, come away,
For it is a pleasant day!

Mother Goose Rhyme

In children we find the essence
of joy, delight and wonder.
A child's smile holds all these things and more.
It is like a caress from the loving hand of God.

Rose Herriges

You make me glad
by your deeds, O Lord;
I sing for joy at the works
of your hands.

Psalm 92:4

All This and More

God made the sunlight,

but it cannot laugh,

God made the moonbeams,

but they cannot smile;

God made the stars,

but they cannot play;

God made the birds,

but they cannot hold the heart;

God made music,

but it cannot love.

So, God made you, my child.

Dorcas S. Miller

Welcome to the world,
little one!
You are truly a sunbeam
in our lives!

I think God gives the children,

as through the land they go,

The most delightful mission

that anyone can know.

He wants us to be sunbeams of love

and hope and cheer,

To brighten up the shadows

that often gather here.

O we are little sunbeams,

sent down from God to man;

In all life's shady places,

we shine as best we can.

Eben Eugene Rexford

How did you come to me, my sweet?
From the land that no man knows?
Did Mr. Stork bring you here on his wings?
Were you born in the heart of a rose?

Did an angel fly with you down from the sky?
Were you found in a gooseberry patch?
Did a fairy bring you from fairyland
To my door—that was left on a latch?

No—my darling was born of a wonderful love,
A love that was Daddy's and mine.
A love that was human, but deep and profound,
A love that was almost divine.

Olga Petrova

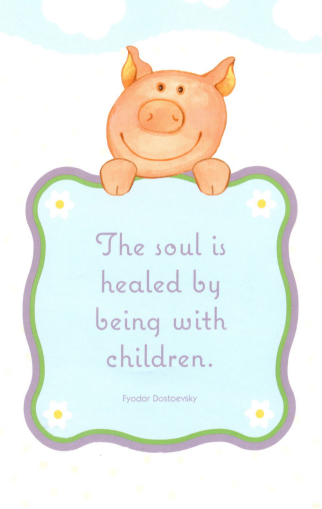

The soul is healed by being with children.

Fyodor Dostoevsky

All Through the Night

Sleep, my babe, lie still and slumber,

All through the night,

Guardian angels God will lend thee,

All through the night;

Soft and drowsy hours are creeping,

Hill and vale in slumber sleeping,

Mother dear her watch is keeping,

All through the night.

Jesus said, "See that you do not look down
on one of these little ones. For I tell you that their
angels in heaven always see the face
of my Father in heaven."

Matthew 18:10

The Lord will command his angels concerning you
to guard you in all your ways;
they will lift you up in their hands,
so that you will not strike your foot against a stone.

Psalm 91:11–12

The Lord will not let your foot slip—
he who watches over you will not slumber.

Psalm 121:3

The Lord bless you
and keep you;
the Lord make his face
shine upon you
and be gracious to you;
the Lord turn his face
toward you
and give you peace.

Numbers 6:24–26